Matthew 28: 1-7

After the Sabbath, at dawn on the first day of the week, Mary Magdalene and the other Mary went to look at the tomb.

There was a violent earthquake, for an angel of the Lord came down from heaven and, going to the tomb, rolled back the stone and sat on it. His appearance was like lightning, and his clothes were white as snow. The guards were so afraid of him that they shook and became like dead men.

The angel said to the women,

"Do not be afraid, for I know that you are looking for Jesus, who was crucified. He is not here; he has risen, just as he said. Come and see the place where he lay. Then go quickly and tell his disciples: 'He has risen from the dead and is going ahead of you into Galilee. There you will see him.' Now I have told you."

Jesus sat on the little donkey and together with His friends He headed toward the city of Jerusalem. Crowds of people stood along the side of the road.

They waved large palm branches and shouted, "Hosanna! Blessed is He who comes in the name of the Lord!"

On Monday, Jesus went into the temple in Jerusalem. He became very angry because the crowds of people were buying and selling animals—the people were not worshipping God.

So Jesus turned over their tables and made the buyers and sellers leave the temple.
The religious leaders were upset with Jesus.

7

On Thursday evening, Jesus and His twelve disciples celebrated the Passover together. During the me
Jesus took some bread, prayed, and then gave some to His friends.

his is my body," He said, "which will be broken." Then Jesus took the cup of wine, prayed, and gave
me to His friends. "This is my blood," he said. "I am giving you a new commandment: Love one
other so that everyone will know you are my disciples."

After the Passover meal, Jesus and His friends went into a nearby garden. "Stay here and pray," Jesus said. "Please stay awake and pray for Me." Jesus walked further into the garden, knelt on the ground and began to pray. "Father, I am willing to do what You want," Jesus said.

oon a group of people and soldiers came through the garden carrying torches. Judas, one of Jesus'
osest friends, was leading the way. The religious leaders gave him thirty pieces of silver to take them
Jesus. The soldiers arrested Jesus.

The soldiers and religious leaders took Jesus to Pontius Pilate, a governor and a judge. Many people lied to the judge about things Jesus had said and done. "I find no wrong in this man. Let Jesus go," said Pilate. But the crowd insisted that Jesus be crucified. Even though Pilate did not agree, he listened to the crowd.

Jesus was silent as the soldiers took Him away. They put a crown made of thorns on Jesus' head. The soldiers nailed Jesus to a cross. Jesus was heard praying, "Father, forgive them." Even though it was daytime, the skies grew dark for three hours. Jesus said in a loud voice, "It is finished!" and then He died.

Friends of Jesus placed His body in a tomb. A large stone was rolled in front of the entrance. Soldiers guarded the tomb so that no one would take Jesus' body.

On Sunday morning, two women both named Mary came to the tomb. They found the stone rolled away from the entrance. An angel sitting on the stone said, "Jesus is not here! He is alive! Go quickly and tell His friends!" The women ran back to the others!

Jesus is alive! He is risen!" shouted the women. The friends did not believe the women! Peter, one of Jesus' closest friends, ran to the tomb. He looked inside and found only the cloths that had wrapped Jesus' body!

Later that day, Jesus joined two of his friends while they walked along the road to a little village. Then, Jesus visited the disciples in Jerusalem. He showed them his nail-scarred hands and feet! It was true—Jesus was alive!

How Much Does God Love Me?

Follow these simple steps and discover how much God Loves you!

 Fold down the top left corner of a piece of paper.

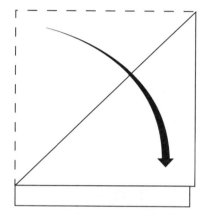

 Then fold down the top right corner.

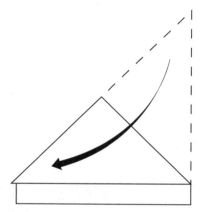

 Fold the left side over the right side.

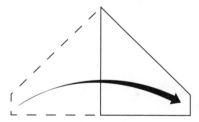

 Cut the paper along the fold line—about one-inch away from the fold.

cut

discard

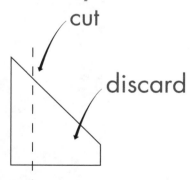

 Carefully open the folded sheet.

Read Romans 5:8 in your Bible.

17

Stained Glass Cross

Plan ahead to make a beautiful reminder of Jesus' death on a cross. You will need clear adhesive-backed paper and multi-colored tissue paper. Place the adhesive-backed paper sticky side up on a table, taping it in place if necessary. Tear tissue paper into small pieces and stick them to the adhesive-backed paper, covering the center. When the center is covered with tissue paper, cover it with another piece of clear adhesive-backed paper—sandwiching the tissue in between.

To make a frame, cut out the shape of a cross from a piece of dark construction paper. Tape the stained glass cross to the back of the construction paper, making certain the beautiful colors show through the cross-shaped opening.

Display the cross where every family member will see it often. Perhaps, every family member can make one to display in a bedroom, kitchen, car, office—wherever it will be seen each day.

Jesus Is The King

Luke 19:28-38

© 2005 Twin Sisters IP, LLC. All Rights Reserved.

Jesus sent two friends into the city. They found a donkey and a colt.

3

I will treat Jesus like a king, too.

8

Many people waved palm branches.

6

Jesus and His friends were traveling to Jerusalem.

2

They took the animals to Jesus. He sat on the donkey and rode into town.

4

The people shouted, "Hosanna!" The people treated Jesus like a king.

7

A large crowd of people came to see Jesus.

5

FOLD

FOLD

Jesus Died On A Cross
Mark 15:16-39

FOLD

FOLD

Many people laughed at Jesus. They did not know He was God's Son.

3

"Jesus is God's Son," they said.

8

His friends were sad. They did not understand why Jesus was dying.

6

Men put Jesus on a cross to die. Jesus had not done anything wrong.

2

Jesus talked to God. "Forgive these people," He said.

4

They put His body in the ground. They sealed the tomb.

7

Jesus still loved the people.

5

Jesus Is Alive!
John 20:1-20

Mary looked inside the tomb.
Jesus was not inside. Mary cried.

3

FOLD

FOLD

Soon, Jesus spoke to His other friends.
Jesus was alive!

8

"Mary!" the man said.
"Jesus!" said Mary.

6

Early Sunday morning Mary came to Jesus' tomb. An angel had rolled away the stone.

2

Mary saw a man in the garden. "Why are you crying?" He asked.

4

Jesus was alive again!

7

"Someone has taken Jesus' body away," said Mary.

5

FOLD

FOLD

Color Code

Color in only the boxes with a ▢ or ●.
The remaining boxes will reveal how much God loves you.

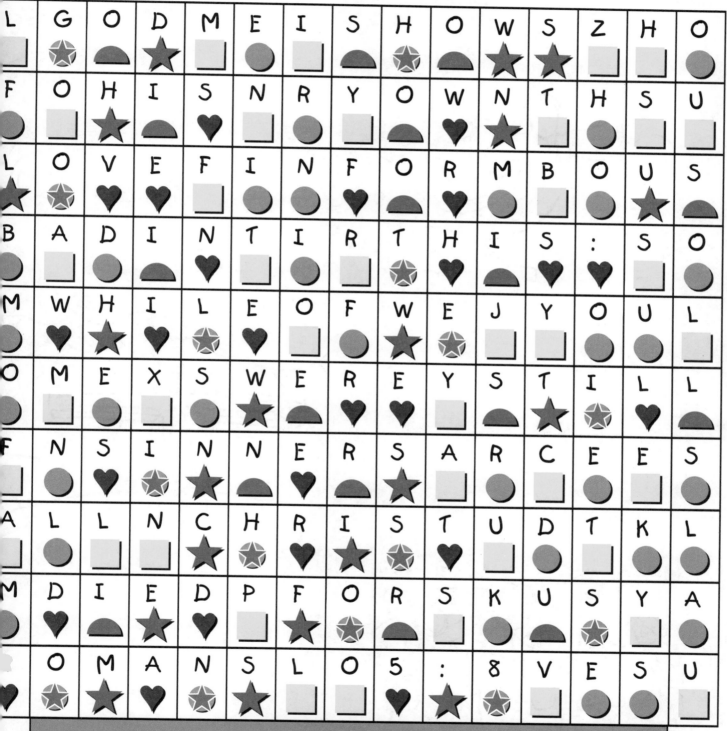

25

What Happened Next?

Tell what is happening in each picture. Draw a circle around the picture that shows wh[at]
happened first. Draw a square around the picture that shows what happened next. The[n]
draw a triangle around the picture that shows what happened last.

Easter Story Cookies

The process of baking these cookies will deepen every family member's understanding of the Resurrection. Easter Story Cookies may very well become a family tradition first for your child, and perhaps his or her children someday.

On the Saturday before Easter collect the following:

You Will Need:

- 1-Cup whole pecans
- 3 Egg whites
- 1-Cup sugar
- 1-Teaspoon vinegar
- Pinch of salt
- Cookie sheet
- Wooden spoon
- Hand mixer
- Mixing bowl
- Wax paper
- Resealable plastic storage bag
- Masking tape
- Family Bible

Preheat oven to 300 degrees F.

Place the pecans in a resealable plastic storage bag and let your child beat them with the spoon to crush them into small pieces. Explain that after Jesus was arrested the Roman soldiers beat Him.
Read John 19:1-3

Help your child smell the vinegar. Put 1-Teaspoon into the mixing bowl. Explain that Jesus was given vinegar to drink while on the cross.
Read John 19:28-30

Add the egg whites to vinegar. Explain that eggs give life. Explain that Jesus gave His life to give us eternal life.
Read John 10:10-11.

Sprinkle a little salt into your child's hand and let her taste it. Pour the remaining salt into the mixing bowl. Explain that this represents the salty tears Jesus' followers shed.
Read Luke 23:27.

Explain that the ingredients so far have not been very tasty.

Add 1-Cup sugar to the mixture. Explain the sweetest part of the whole story is that Jesus died because He loves us. He wants you and your child to know and belong to Him.
Read Psalm 34:8 and John 3:16.

Beat the mixture on high speed for 12-15 minutes until stiff peaks are formed. Explain that the color white represents the purity in God's eyes of those whose sins have been forgiven by Jesus.
Read Isaiah 1:18 and John 3:1-3.

Fold in the crushed, broken nuts. Drop the cookie dough by teaspoons onto a cookie sheet covered with wax paper. Explain that each mound represents the tomb where Jesus' body was placed.
Read Matthew 27:57-60.

Carefully put the cookie sheet in the oven, close the door, and turn the oven OFF. Give the children masking tape and help them seal the oven door. Be careful—the edges of the oven may still be extremely hot!! Explain that Jesus' tomb was sealed.
Read Matthew 27:65-66.

Go to bed. Explain that Jesus' followers were in despair when the tomb was sealed.
Read John 16:20 and 22.

On Easter morning, before the children awaken, remove the tape from the oven door. Allow the children to open the oven and to give everyone a cookie. Point out the cracked surface and take a bite. The cookies are hollow! Explain that on the first Easter Jesus' followers were amazed to find the tomb open and empty!
Read Matthew 28:1-9.

Participate in the Easter worship celebration at your church knowing that your family already has an understanding of the message.

Word Search

Find and circle the following words.

JESUS   ANGEL   DIED   ALIVE
DISCIPLES   SOLDIERS   CROSS   TOMB

```
Z  T  U  I  L  H  J  S  A
T  O  M  B  A  D  E  F  M
C  F  D  Y  Z  L  S  Y  S
A  L  I  V  E  D  U  C  O
N  S  P  C  R  O  S  S  L
G  H  H  L  U  D  D  E  D
E  M  Q  U  S  I  A  B  I
L  S  A  F  L  E  S  H  E
B  M  A  B  Y  D  U  E  R
D  I  S  C  I  P  L  E  S
```

Hosanna!

They took palm branches and went out to meet him, shouting, "Hosanna!" "Blessed is he who comes in the name of the Lord!" John 12:13

Finish drawing the palm branch.

The Empty Tomb

So Peter and the other disciple started for the tomb. Both were running, but the other disciple outran Peter and reached the tomb first. John 20:3-4

Help Peter and the other disciple run to Jesus' tomb.

Start

Why Do You Look For The Living Among The Dead?

Unscramble each word to learn what the angel said to the women!

‾‾ ‾‾   ‾‾ ‾‾   ‾‾ ‾‾ ‾‾   ‾‾ ‾‾ ‾‾ ‾‾

E H   S I   T N O   R E H E.

‾‾ ‾‾   ‾‾ ‾‾ ‾‾   ‾‾ ‾‾ ‾‾ ‾‾ ‾‾

E H   S H A   S I N E R !

Answer: He is not here. He has risen!

...He was taken up before their very eyes, and a cloud hid him from their sight. They were looking intently up into the sky as he was going, when suddenly two men dressed in white stood beside them. "Men of Galilee," they said, "why do you stand here looking into the sky? This same Jesus, who has been taken from you into heaven, will come back in the same way you have seen him go into heaven."
Acts 1:9-11